Thatch in and around Ryedale

by

E. Blizzard, N. Sykes
W. Tegetmeir and M. Watts

Ryedale Folk Museum
&
Hutton Press Ltd.
2000

Published by

The Ryedale Folk Museum
Hutton-le-Hole, York YO62 6UA

and

The Hutton Press Ltd.
130 Canada Drive, Cherry Burton,
Beverley, East Yorkshire, HU17 7SB

Printed and bound by
The College Press,
a division of the University of Hull

ISBN 1 902709 06 3

Tony and Joe Hurst Memorial

This is the first book to be published in memory of Tony and Joe Hurst, who contributed so much to the Ryedale Folk Museum, thanks to the generosity of their family and friends from near and far.

Yorventure recognises Ryedale Folk Museum's role as an important local and regional resource, and is pleased to be funding the restoration of the thatch on Stang End Cottage through the landfill tax credit scheme.

The land fill tax credit scheme allows landfill site operators to invest some of the tax collected on waste in environmental projects near to landfill sites.

Since 1997 Yorventure has committed nearly £2 million to environmental projects throughout North Yorkshire via the landfill tax credit scheme. This funding has helped provide and improve local amenities such as village halls and play facilities. It has helped to fund major conservation work, nature reserves and the creation and restoration of woodland. It has also provided funding for innovative education and research projects into sustainable waste management.

I wish Ryedale Folk Museum every success with its work on Thatching and its continued efforts in communicating the social history of this part of Yorkshire.

John Kilner
Yorventure Project manager

Yorventure receives funding from Yorwaste Ltd
via the landfill tax credit scheme.

Contents

An old turf walled stable with a roughly thatched roof photographed at the turn of the century. This is an example of the construction methods used by the very poorest people for hundreds of years. Photo W.Hayes. RFM4885.

THATCH in and around RYEDALE

For more than a thousand years thatched cottages have been a familiar sight throughout the North York Moors where they are traditionally - but not exclusively - associated with single-storey cruck framed dwellings. Across the north they have all but vanished - except for the remaining core in and near Ryedale where about 40 survive today - by far the largest concentration in north eastern England.

HISTORY of LOCAL THATCH

The origin of thatched roofs is lost in the mists of antiquity and because thatching was so familiar written records are few and far between. The Venerable Bede of Durham who died in 735 described dwellings with roofs of thatch, and the Anglo Saxons who established forerunners of Ryedale's existing villages gathered local vegetation with which to roof their dwellings. Their legacy continues in such names as Thackside (in Newtondale) derived from thaksike - Old Norse for 'the stream with thatching reed'.

A familiar local name - Thackray - described a man who thatched with reeds. Originally the word 'thack' referred to any roof covering because vegetation was so widely used, and early stone tiles were known as 'thackstones'. A 15th century building account for York Minster lists 'thackburdes' meaning boards upon which a lead roof was to be laid. Outbuildings of Pickering Castle were heather thatched.

Among the main factors contibuting to survival of thatched cottages hereabouts are a particular **local building style** and a tradition of large **estate land ownership**.

Local Tradition

Historically the region was well endowed with sturdy albeit shortish oak trees - ideal for the making of crucks. From the ancient royal forest of Pickering which extended over much of todays moorland, large curved timbers were felled and either split lengthwise or matched in pairs to create crucks. The timbers were joined at the apex by a saddle, midway by a collar beam and at eave level by a tie beam to form an A-shaped frame or cruck which supported the roof (but not the walls) and determined the size of building. Erected between 10 and 16 feet apart, the crucks carried a rough-hewn ridge pole and purlins on which rafters were secured to create a base for thatch. The width and height of the building depended upon the shape and ground level span of crucks; length was determined by the number of crucks and bays constructed and could be altered as needed, often extended to create animal housing. Stone for walls and local seaves (rushes), bracken, ling or straw to cover the roof were all plentiful in this area. Thus a thatched cruck-framed longhouse was the local medieval man's do-it-yourself farmstead. It was cheap, simple to build yet afforded adequate shelter for man and beast.

Across the moors and moorland dales local sandstone provided excellent walling material but where corallian limestone outcrops along the southern fringe, encompassing most of the villages between Helmsley and Ayton, builders had to make do with a less durable rock. This was not a problem for cruck house construction as limestone rubble walls could be replaced without displacing the roof supporting crucks.

In the Middle Ages and 16th century cruck construction was general, even at manor house level. In 1641 George Hicks, then rector of Levisham, was in trouble with the church court for *'suffering the thatch to be blown off from part of the housing belonging to the parsonage and not repairing it'.*
... As villages expanded and more land was brought into cultivation, so more cruck houses went up until the rural upheavals of the 18th century.

Estate Property.

New farming methods along with enclosure of common land and open fields created rising prosperity among a new class of gentry farmers and enterprising landlords who acquired and expanded ancient rural estates. For new buildings pantiles or Welsh and Westmorland slates carried by the new rail network, replaced thatching for roofs. More affluent freeholders upgraded their low and often dark thatched cottages.

But for many people in this area home improvement was not an option. The majority were tenants on large estates not concerned with modernisation of existing humble cottages. Such folk had little choice but to continue living in 'dismal hovels' by todays standards.

Arthur Young, agricultural writer, made his six month tour through the north of England in 1769 and described 'farms on the Duncombe Park estate surprisingly small 20 to 5 acres - the husbandry of these farmers is universally bad - a poor wretched set of people'.

Stone bank in Rosedale a late 19th century photo. The central section of the roof is in good condition but the section over the living end of the cottage is in need of repair. Note the turf stack on the left of the picture. RFM 7386.

In 1800 a land surveyor, John Tuke, reporting to the Board of Agriculture on the state of agriculture in North Yorkshire, wrote *'farmhouses are generally indifferent and insufficient for the farms. . . . .they are mostly thatched with wheat or rye straw.............the practice of thatching the roofs of buildings is far from being economical; this kind of covering being frequently in want of repair .....causes other parts of the building to be injured; it also affords harbour for vermin and is more expensive in the first cost and repairs than pantiles.......the cottages of labourers are generally small and low.......the farmer is by no means well accommodated but the labourer is much worse ....humanity requires that cottages should be built affording habitations more wholesome, comfortable and decent than those we too often see'*.

Thomas Parker, poet, historian and thatcher of Wombleton, describing Helmsley in 1821 wrote *'the houses low and covered with thatch.....what kept the town in that state was the unchangeable mind of the late Lord Feversham, an enemy to pride, extravagance and dress'*. When his successor took over the estate in 1841 it seems there was some improvement although a survey in 1868 shows that of 256 houses in Helmsley, 34 were recently slated, 66 thatched and the remaining 156 tiled. The thatched houses and cottages were well distributed throughout the town and of the 66 no fewer that 45 were *'old or very bad'*. At Pockley 25 out of the 36 houses were thatched including half of the then 10 farmhouses in the township.

Although Kirkbymoorside in 1570 was described as *'a market town inhabyted all with pore people'* the 17th century saw new improved buildings constructed by increasing numbers of owner occupiers and small developers in Kirkbymoorside and Pickering unlike Helmsley and neighbouring villages which continued under estate ownership. In Kirkbymoorside more than one roof has been re-tiled in recent years only to reveal that earlier tiling had been laid on top of original thatch. (A farmhouse south of Wombleton still has ancient thatch beneath its modern pantiles). No thatched dwellings now exist in Pickering and Kirkbymoorside.

Around 1870 surveys of Duncombe estate reveal that in Bilsdale *'most houses were thatched or thatched with tile, some with bad old thatch'*. Bransdale was similarly described. Gillamoor had 13 thatched properties, Kirkbymoorside had a mixture of thatch and tile and Pockley had 26 thatched and several part tiled part thatched. Throughout the estate there were few good or new tiled roofs but many with *'poor old thatch.'*

The original thatch was found underneath the tiles on this house in Kirkbymoorside in 1997. Photo Tony Clark.

A derelict cottage in Goathland. The thatch has all tumbled in and it is typical of the poor quality housing that was replaced in the great rebuilding of the houses and farms that went on throughout the late 18th and early 19th centuries. Photo W.Hayes RFM 4105.

Not surprisingly this situation continued throughout the rural depression years from 1880. Although more dwellings passed into private ownership, especially when the death in the first world war of the heir to the Duncombe estate necessitated an extensive sale. Thatched roofs were still frequent in most villages through the 1920's and 1930's when money was hard to come by for rural people. Not until prosperity returned during and after the second world war did the majority of thatched roofs disappear in widespread house improvement. The numerous 'tin roofs' (corrugate iron sheeting was a cheap covering for decaying thatch) vanished and by 1960 thatched dwellings were few and far between. The Plough Inn at Wombleton lost its thatch in the 1970s when Farndale still had 7 thatched cottages (the dale now has only one left). Carr Cote in Bilsdale fell into dereliction and the Mouse Cottage at Kilburn was re-roofed with tiles. A scarcity value set in. Preservation replaced demolition. At this time a nucleus of old thatched roofs lingered in Pockley (7), Harome (6) and Beadlam (3). A recognised need to conserve these remnants of local history led to their restoration and provided work for a local thatcher to set up in business. Thus the 'dismal hovels' of yesteryears' peasants have taken on a new lease of life as much sought after private homes.

A winters day at Delves Cottage, Egton. C 1950 One half of the roof is still covered in tin over the old thatch . The Thatcher lays latts across the rafters to continue re-thatching. Photo R.Hayes RFM5130. Compare this photo with photo on page 11.

10

Delves Cottage in 1988. Thatched in traditional long straw by William Tegetmeir in 1994.

Present day policy of the North York Moors National Park is to protect remaining thatched cottages by requiring owners to re-roof only with thatch. It seeks to retain the validity of this ancient local style by disallowing any new thatched dwellings. This causes some anomalies as can be seen at Pockley where a new thatched house has been built on the eastern side which lies outside the Park boundary.

The Plough Inn Wombleton 1958. Like many houses in the area this small cruck building has had the thatch replaced with pantiles. Photo R.Hayes RFM 4846.

FIRE HAZARD

When one realises that most humble cottages had no chimneys until Tudor times, it is not surprising that unguarded cooking fires frequently set the roof ablaze and practically every small community valued its thatch-rake used to tear off burning thatch. The Museum's thatch-rake is displayed on the wall opposite the blacksmiths shop. From 11th century onwards one town after another prohibited thatch for new roofs but in rural North Yorkshire roofs continued to be made of cheap and local ling and straw.

A desciption of domestic buildings in Ryedale (Royal Commission on the Houses of the North York Moors 1987) states ' *Much of what existed was swept away by fire. Between 1578 and 1587 forty-six trees were delivered to tenants in the manor of Pickering whose houses were burnt and in 1607 great harm was done by exremity of fire in Helmsley but the grant of £6 13 4d for rebuilding the houses does not suggest anything large or well built. The fire risk was less from the use of timber construction than from thatch, which survived as a roof covering in these towns unil the 20th century.'*

As early as 1212 in London a coating of lime plaster on thatch was made compulsory to reduce combustibility. In the reign of Elizabeth 1 the townspeople of Hull were forbidden *'to theake with straw, reade or hay or otherwise than with thacke tyle'*and its use in towns today is controlled through bye-laws.

When wasps made a nest in a thatched roof covering a cottage in Bondgate, Helmsley, an attempt was made to smoke them out with a red hot poker. The wasps went up in flames - but so did the thatch and much of the cottage!

At Low Bottoms, Thornton Riseborough, a farmhouse and adjacent buildings, all covered in old decayed thatch, were destroyed by fire in 1860. Doubtless many more suffered the same fate as well as a cottage at Sheriff Hutton and Oak Crag, a cottage in Farndale now replaced by a large modern house. At Low Farm,Pockley, some 20 years ago re-thatching and new roof timbers were required after a long dry spell caused sparks to smoulder on the roof.

ROOFING with THATCH

In North Yorkshire centuries ago **seaves** or **rushes** (*Juncus effusus*), bracken (*Pteridium aquilinum*) and **turf** under thatch were basic roofing materials, perhaps because they were so plentiful and free for the taking. Fylingdales manor court stipulated that no commoner should harvest bracken either for thatching or cattle bedding before a specified date, presumably to give everyone a fair chance to collect what they needed. All these materials deteriorated rapidly and turf, dug from the peaty moorland, gave a wet heavy covering unless it was covered by ling.

Yealms or bundles of heather ready for thatching.

Ling or **heather** - (*Calluna vulgaris*) was widely used for thatching and again Fylingdales manor court made sure this was not wasted by decreeing in 1682 that *'none shall burn any thatch linge under pain of 10s 0d every default'*. It was harvested while in flower and laid with the roots entwined and pointing upwards. Ling thatching was widespread on commons and moorland regions where little corn was grown. Although it provided a dark sombre roof, ling was often preferred to straw for its durability and lighter weight. Under the recent straw thatch at Spout House, Bilsdale and elsewhere may be seen remnants of previous ling thatch.

Until the 18th century **rye** (*Secale cereale*) was the main bread crop for Ryedale peasants. It was widely grown and a good deal cheaper than wheat brought by wagons over the moors from Cleveland. The long tough straw of rye was valuable roofing material and is still used when obtainable but wheat flour was deemed more palatable and by about 1780 improved farming methods enabled farmers to grow wheat and oats in preference to rye. Oat straw is too soft for thatching and *'birds would not let it alone'* (Henry Best, East Yorkshire farmer writing in 1641) whereas **wheat** straw remains the most used on re-thatched roofs today.

Common reed (Phragmites australis) is considered the best material for thatching. Also known as water reed, it can last up to 70 years compared with say 20 years for wheat and 30 years for rye straw, but its rigidity makes it unsuitable for capping the ridge which is usually done with wheat straw. Because it is not easily available in this part of the country today reed harvested in Tayside, Norfolk and Hampshire is used as well as European imports from Hungary, Austria, France and Turkey. This adds greatly to the cost of a reed thatch - £10,000 for a complete new roof as compared with £1,000 for tiles. It may be that in times past, before the draining of the plain of York and the Vale of Pickering, there would have been sufficient marshland to provide for local needs.

Wheat (Triticum sp) is the material most often used today. Long unbroken straw is essential for thatching with varieties such as Maris huntsman and Maris widgeon favoured. With the advent of combine harvesters after the second world war new short strawed varieties of corn were grown and the thatcher had to look elsewhere for straw grown specially for thatching. A farm at Holme-on-Spalding Moor in East Yorkshire and another near Wakefield grow and traditionally harvest this unusual crop.

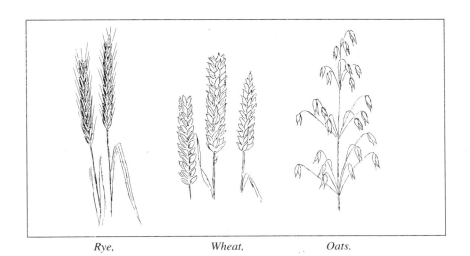

Rye,　　　　　　　*Wheat,*　　　　　*Oats.*

COST OF THATCHING

Middleton churchwardens' accounts indicate the ongoing cost of thatch and its replacement by slates with tile ridges.

1745 thatching the vestry		2	6d
1747 to the thatcher		1	0
serving the thatcher			6
1748 straw thatching and attendance		3	1
1749 for 3 threaves of straw		1	6
for thatching, pulling and serving		1	8
1754 vestry thatching		3	6
1756 thatch		6	0
the thatcher		1	6
for serving			6
1758for thatching vestry			8
15 logs straw		1	6
serving thatcher			6
1759 for straw and thatching vestry		2	10
1790 1 ton & 26 st of Blue Slate	4	4	6
1793 slates and tiling		1	3
1796 six slates		1	6
1808 blue slates to porch		2	6

In 1800 Goathland Overseer paid out to thatch the village poor house:

pulling 50 threaves of ling	16	8d
thatching 5 days @ 2s6d a day	12	6
3 threaves straw @ 1s6d each	4	6
tar band and going to Whitby to get laths	4	2
serving thatcher 5 days @ 2s a day	10	0
lowance for thatcher and man	2	2
mason	£5 19	3
glazing	5	10

The old pauper house had first been taken down for 15 shilling by Jonathan Robinson, stone mason. He gives its dimensions 30ft long x 15ft wide, one storey high and with a partition wall making it into two rooms and had been thatched with a mixture of straw and ling.

Levisham Pauper book also records the cost and use of thatch in the early 19th century.

1829/3	*12 threave thatch @ 2s per threave*	£1 4	0d
	thatcher work 2 days @ 2/6 per day	5	0d
	server 1 day	1	6d
	thatch steeping	2	0d
1833/4	*for Margaret Gib house thatching 24 threave*		
	straw @ 2/-	£2 8	0d
	thatcher 6 days @ 1/3 per day	7	6d
	server 6 days @ 1/- per day	6	0d
	thatcher meat 6 days @ 1/- per day	6	0d
	server ditto	6	0d
	steeping the thatch	3	0d
1847/8	*straw for William Dixon house 20 threave*		
	@ 2/6	£2 10	0d
	thatcher wages and meat 5 days @		
	3/3 per day	16	3d
	serving thatcher 4 and a half days @ 1/9	7	9d
	steeping straw	3	0d
	tiles and putting on	2	0d

It is interesting to note the inclusion of tiling alongside thatching in the later entry.

A century later an account shows:

1937/8	*Stang End farm,, Danby:*			
	30 cwt wheat straw from Horse Close			
	farm and cartage	*4*	*2*	*6d*
	Preparing straw and thatching 55 hours			
	@ 11d per hour	*£2*	*10*	*5*
1960	A re-thatch at Old Malton had taken			
	5 tons of straw and cost £200.			
1998	Re-thatching White Cottage at the Folk Museum cost			
	£9000 in 1999			

PANTILES

From about 1740 tiles had been imported at Whitby where a tilery was eventually established; pantiles were also made at Black Bull near Pickering and at Cropton. Tilehouse Bridge over the Hodge beck near Welburn is said to take its name from a tile factory, and north of Rievaulx the farm name Tylas may be corrupted from tilehouse. The novelty - and considered superiority - of having a pantiled roof is reflected in the numerous dwellings called Red House in this area. Nevertheless, parsonage terriers (accounts) relate continued use of thatch on new and restored parsonages into the 19th century. In 1777 Sleights chapelry built new property of stone and thatch but by 1857 they were tiled.

Lockton manor house remained thatched until it became derelict and was demolished early in the 20th century. In 1757 when Quakers riding to the meeting house at Hutton le Hole needed to graze and stable their horses on a Sunday their yearly rent was seven threaves or a day's thatching straw. The Friends Meeting House at 79 West End, Kirkbymoorside was thatched from 1690 until 1798.

And not everyone was convinced that tiles formed a better roof than thatch. Ralph Ward of Guisborough re-roofed his house with tiles in 1755 but in the winter his diary relates *'came a great rain which poweres in every room in all my houseing and ran into many low roomes in a dismal manner'*. He pulled the tiles off his sheephouse and re-covered it with thatch to provide better insulation. People living in thatched cottages today often comment on its excellent insulation. 'We don't need central heating' remarked one owner, adding that when old thatch was being trimmed to make way for a new covering, rain had penetrated only a couple of inches of the 2 to 3 feet of old straw.

CARING FOR THATCH

Patching some holes in a roof in West End Kirkbymoorside. The man working on the roof is using a swallow tail to stob in some holes. Judging by the precarious nature of the ladder propped on the wheelbarrow this could well be the owner of the house rather than a professional thatcher. Many people would have patched and mended their own roofs. Photo W.Lealman RFM 7033.

Constant repair and renewal has gone on for generations. It is common to see layering 2 to 3 feet thick under eaves of a thatched roof where new coverings have been laid on top of old. A recently thatched dwelling in Bilsdale had accumulated layers of turf, ling, tin and straw up to 6 feet thick which had broken underlying timbers with the weight. Rats can be a problem in thatched roofs. Two owners described how they keep traps ready and watch constantly for signs of rat runs.

Before common use of bank savings accounts, thatch provided a secret haven for valuables. The truth of Thomas Parker's lines *'Their money bags in the thatch was hid with careful thought'* was brought to light when a hoard of sovereigns was discovered in a Bransdale farmhouse roof and again when a valuable silver spoon fell from old thatch as Harome Manor house was being taken down before transportation to the Museum. In recent years a crowbar and a small pair of spats have been added to treasures discovered in Ryedale thatch. Reminder of a strong belief in evil spirits came to light in 1998 when local re-thatching revealed the mummified remains of a cat and kittens secreted in a roof. In deference to this widely held folklore the remains were replaced under the new thatch - the mischievous Hob cannot be allowed to re-appear in the new millennium!.

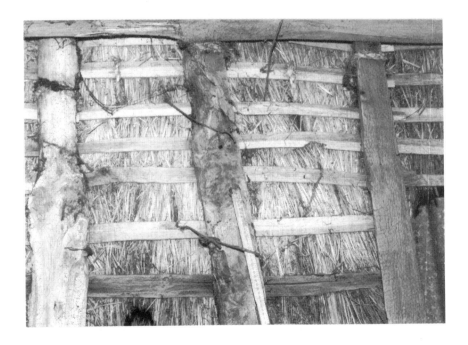

The underside of a thatched roof at Southfield House Rosedale. This thatch is at least 70 years old and could be over a 100 years old. The straw rope and the riven latts roughly laid across the rafters can still be seen. Photo Stephen Haigh ,Ed Dennison Archaeological Services.

To shed water quickly, thatch requires a minimum 45 degrees pitch, steeper than pantiles and although many formerly thatched roofs have been raised and given an easier pitch, in this area pantiles have often replaced thatch without alteration to the roof. This is often the case with cruck houses where the roof pitch is determined by the curvature of the crucks. As new types of roof truss replaced crucks, tiles or slates proved more suitable.

Not suprisingly, thatching and the making of besoms (brooms made from ling) were often carried out by the same family.

Three magnificent corn stacks on a farm at Skiplam Grange c 1911. Photo W.Hayes RFM 1677.

THATCH on CORN and HAY RICKS

Until well after the second world war most farmers stored their corn in small circular stacks, thatched to await threshing day. They were built about 6ft high to the eaves tapering up another 3ft or so -each one just enough for one days threshing intermittently through the winter. This continued in some areas until the combine harvester took over completely in the 1960's and it was a popular Sunday occupation to walk round neighbouring farms inspecting the various stacks. Those on the roadside always received that bit extra care! As farming improvements got underway in the 19th century competitions on a par with hedge-laying and ploughing flourished and different dales developed localised styles of stacking and thatching. As they were not intended to last more than a few months at most, corn and hayricks received only a thin covering of thatch, and from a practical standpoint ample overhang was left at the eaves to minimise rain penetrating the stack from below. But where stacks were to be judged competitively or viewed over-critically by neighbours more meticulous shaving was carried out. The finishing touch added by practised thatchers was an ornate corn dolly at the top.

A notice in the Malton Messenger of September 1856 claimed that William Richardson could be matched to thatch and stack either against the Little Fryup 'Brag' or the Great Fryup 'Pet'.

THATCHERS

When thatching was commonplace most farm workers learned the skill and to this day repairing thatch is occasionally done by an owner. But with the mechanisation of farm work only specialists acquired the skill to re-thatch a whole roof.

Anthony Stonehouse who grew up in Farndale, is recorded in Lastingham parish documents in 1835 as a thatcher. This is unusual because at that time thatching was not considered a specialist job unlike the straw-maker, basket-maker, yeast-maker, clairvoyant, clog-maker, match-maker, masons, joiners and gardeners who are listed in local 19th century directories.

Small farms (often less than 20 acres) and scattered hamlets forced farm workers to be skilled in all trades - including thatching. Craftsmen with thatching, hedge-laying, shearing or mowing skills often moved away to the Wolds and Vale of Mowbray for seasonal work, returning to local farms for the later harvest.

Thomas Parker lived at Fenwick House, Wombleton and acquired local fame as a poet, antiquarian and thatcher. He was born in 1812 in Wombleton, the third of six brothers and sisters. He was an outspoken critic of the church, mourned the loss of ancient buildings and families, and felt there was still a need for the stocks and whipping posts. He was a keen historian and compiled a lengthy history of Kirkdale and nearby villages in which he describes an old manor house in Welburn; *'the original part of this house was roofed with mighty timber and thatched nearly to the ground, and the enteriour with wide chimneys and Randle bokes, with long swinging Pothooks which reached to the hearth that was heaped high with turf from Rallgate Moor. This homely Mansion was pulled down in the year 1861'.*

Thomas Parker of Wombleton , Poet, Antiquary, Historian and Thatcher.

George Lawson of Harome continued thatching later in the 19th century but his son Thomas apparently shunned his father's craft and instead became a tailor's apprentice.

Jack Lumsden holding an easing knife and Swallow tail on a roof in Farndale, note the hobnailed boots and protective sacking tied around his knees. RFM 2700. See also drawing on page 31.

Jack Lumsden of Farndale, a local bandsman of some repute, was the local thatcher in 1926. Working with ling gathered from the surrounding moors and straw, he 'stobbed' everything and was the last local 'stobber'. He combined thatching jobs along with running a farm and walked over the moors from Farndale to Bilsdale to thatch the old Sun Inn. Maybe that was his last thatching job because a sack containing his original thatching tools still hangs in a Bilsdale barn.

Seth Eccles of Helmsley worked for Handleys, a local builder, and often had to turn his hand to thatching. He travelled around on a moped while his employer transported his tools and undertook the estimating. Seth's work included various buildings on York racecourse and he took the opportunity to expand his skill when offered training by the Rural Industries Bureau after the second world war. He worked entirely with long straw, never using reed. He died in 1997.

Seth Eccles working at the Ryedale Folk Museum Photo T.Geoffrey Willey.

William Tegetmeier lived in a thatched cottage in Wiltshire before starting work as a painter and decorator. When he moved to Yorkshire in the early 1970's and discovered that Seth Eccles was about to retire he saw an opportunity to follow in his stead. He bought thatching tools from Seth and went on a training course run by the Council of Small Industries in Rural Areas (CoSIRA) As well as working on the diminished number of thatched cottages in Ryedale, William now travels across the country and has an order book for months ahead. The new thatch on the Museum's old cottages are examples of his craft

Other 20th century Ryedale thatchers were **'Stamper' Dowkes** of Pockley and **John Ventress** of Skiplam.

Christopher Smart has recently moved to Hovingham and is hoping to find adequate work in the north east. Early in 1999 he started a re-thatch on the Star Inn at Harome.

THATCHING TODAY

Thatching involves fixings bundles of vegetation to a roof to form a water proof layer .The rain is shed from a thatched roof by the water running down the lengths of the straw. A well thatched roof will only be wet to a depth of a couple of inches. How the bundles are arranged and how they are fixed depends on the materials being used, the style of the roof being covered and whether the roof is being thatched from scratch or a fresh layer is being added to an existing old thatch. Apart from the technique of stobbing(see below) traditionally all the roofs in the area covered by this book were thatched either in long straw or heather.

Preparing the materials for a long straw roof.

Today special long stemmed varieties of wheat and rye are grown especially for thatching and it is reaped in such a way as to preserve the length of the straw and to not crush it or unduly bend it. It is delivered to the site in large bundles known as loggins, with all the stalks pointing the same way. If the straw has been harvested sometime ago and has become brittle it is sometimes steeped in water.

A loggin of wheat straw as delivered to the site. William Tegetmeier working at the museum.

The bundles of straw used to actually thatch the roof are known as yealms and are prepared from the loggins. The loggins are opened up and spread out in a line approximately 20 yards long to a depth of 2 or 3 feet. A thatcher pulls out handfuls until they have a comfortable amount of straw to carry onto the roof. All the stalks of the straw in the yealm are lying parallel to each other. Many thatchers tie a piece of string or a twist of straw rope around each yealm for ease of carrying.

The loggins have been laid in a row under the blue sheet and William Tegetmeir pulls handfulls of straw to make a yealm.

The finished yealms ready to be used on the roof.

As much as a third of the work involved in thatching a roof is spent preparing the materials.

Making spars, splitting the hazel sticks.

One of the longest jobs is making the spars. Spars are used to fix the yealms to the roof.

The finished spar twisted in the middle and bent into a hairpin shape.

There are over 40 different local names for spars echoing the many regional styles and traditions of thatching. A spar is essentially a wooden hairpin approximately 12 to 18 inches long. These are made in advance often during the cold and wet winter months. Two to three foot lengths of coppice wood, often hazel or willow are cut each one being between an inch and a half and two inches thick. These are then split down their length several times to produce between 3 and 4 thinner lengths. Shortly before their use they are deftly twisted and folded into a 'U ' or hairpin shape. The twisting stops them breaking in half when being bent into shape and creates an outward pressure on the two legs of the 'U' that helps to hold them in place on the roof. Hundreds of spars are need to thatch even a small roof.

The roof Structure.

A thatched roof has to have a steep pitch to ensure that the rain is shed quickly. Although many different pitches have been thatched an angle of at least 50 degrees is preferable. The existence of a steeply pitched tile roof can sometimes be evidence that it was once thatched especially if additional courses of stonework have been added to the top of the wall. The main structural timbers for thatched and tiled roofs are the same. However instead of tile latts that have to be sawn straight and nailed on precisely, the thatcher could tie or nail coppice wood poles at rough intervals to tie the yealms onto. Unlike tile and slate roofs the ridge board on a thatched roof is much taller and sticks up above the ends of the rafters in order to give support to the ridge thatch.

Thatching the roof.

You begin to thatch at a bottom corner of the roof. The first yealm bisects the right angle and you continue along the eaves from left to right for a given length, usually what can be comfortably reached from the ladder without moving it. This is known as a stulch or breed. The straw is held in place by tying a rod on top of it and holding it down with spars pushed tightly into the thatch. It is usually necessary to hammer the spars in with a wooden mallet. The next row of yealms will overlap the first row by over half its length; this is continued right up to the ridge. For the gables a more wedge shaped yealm is prepared. They are placed at an angle to the gable but pointing down the roof so that when trimmed only the ends of the stalks will be seen. The last row of yealms on the sides of the roof have their tops in line with the ridge. A stout rope or ridge roll of straw 6 to 8 inches in diameter is made up and laid along the ridge. This is then covered with another double ended yealm straddling the apex. It is necessary to build up a considerable depth of straw on the ridge to ensure the roof is water tight. This can be two feet deep in contrast to the sides of the roof, which will be between 9 and 12 inches deep.

Starting a roof. The double layer of yealms is tied onto latts that are laid at right angles on the rafters.

A ridge roll of heather with a pitchfork.

Finishing off.

When the thatch is fixed on the thatcher can then straighten the straw with a rake. This is done after each vertical strip,or stulch has been laid. Finally when all the thatch is laid the overhanging straw on the gables and eaves is trimmed with an easing knife. Easing knives were often razor sharp scythe blades mounted on a short handle. The angle at which this final trimming or easing is cut depends on the taste of the customer, local custom or opinion of the thatcher.

Seth Eccles using an easing knife to trim the eaves on Oak Cragg Farndale 1963. RFM 126.

In the North Yorkshire area and elsewhere external rows of rods or liggers, held in position with spars, are used along the gables and the ridge to provide extra strength for these sections most prone to wind damage. These external fixings are often laid in a zigzag decorative pattern. In some parts of the country the ridge straw itself is shaped into decorative patterns. It appears that this has not been a traditional practice in North Yorkshire although today some cutomers ask for it to be done. When thatching with reed it is found to be too tough and unbending a material and more pliable wheat straw is used to form the ridge, (an exception to this practice can be seen at Runswick Bay where the salt air would have caused rapid deterioration of wheat straw.)

Finally some thatchers add a finishing touch by fixing straw models, often pheasants or owls onto the ridge. Early photographs show no evidence of this being done in North Yorkshire. These may have been an attempt to scare away unwanted small birds.

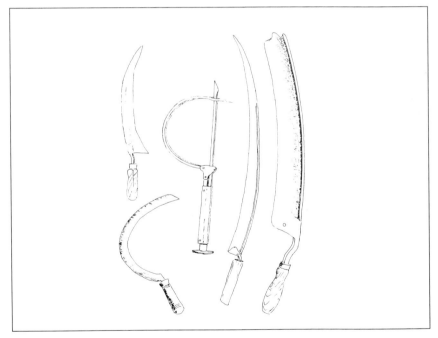

Thatching tools. Short easing knife, sickle, stitching needle and two easing knifes. This easing knife can be seen in use by Jack Lumsden in photo on page 23.

Thatching a roof for the first time.

In the past some new roofs, or roofs that for one reason or another were stripped down to the bare roof timbers, had strips of turf laid at right angles to the main roof spars, or rafters. These strips of turf were about 9 inches wide, two inches thick and up to three feet long and cut with a turf spade. They were laid soil side upper most each strip overlapping the one below. Turf provided a good surface for the spars to grip in. This method went out of fashion at least a hundred years ago because the turf tended to disintegrate and drop bits onto people below. This was especially unsatisfactory when there was no ceiling. Also when using turf the main rafters have to be relatively closer together to support the turf. When turf is not being used the main rafters can be further apart and thin latts or poles fixed at right angles to the rafters for the straw to be supported on and attached to.

Thatching with turf and heather at the Ryedale Folk Museum. The turf replaces the need for latts but the rafters need to be closer together.

When thatching a roof for the first time without turf it is necessary to tie or nail the rods and yealms in place, because there is no existing depth of old straw to grip the spars. When tying on, a long thatchers needle is used. The thatcher threads a length of tarred string or twisted straw rope onto the end of the needle and pushes it right through the thatch and reaching under the yealm to be attached wraps it around the yealm and ties it to the latt or rafter.

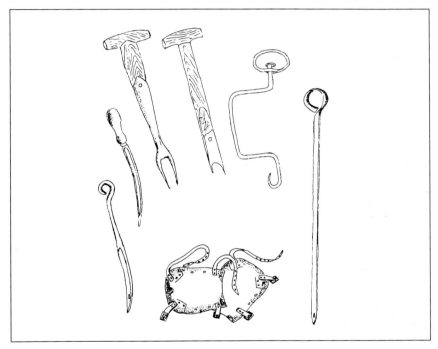

Thatching tools. l to r. 2 short needles, swallow tails, straw band winder, two long needles and a pair of knee pads.

Straw ropes were made with straw band winders. This resembles a brace and bit, with a hook on the end instead of a bit. One person turns the winder holding it tightly into their midriff, the other person puts a wisp of straw over the hook and continues to feed wisps one into another much as a spinster feeds wool on a spinning wheel. This person walks slowly backwards as the rope gets longer. If nails are used they are made especially for the job and are approximately 9 inches long with a hook at the end.

Heather thatch.

Thatching with heather requires the same techniques as straw with one or two exceptions. Heather yealms are often prepared by forking the heather into shape with a pitchfork. Heather is much harsher to work with but will last longer. Heather thatched roofs can be seen in the Ryedale Folk Museum.

Stobbing.

Stobbing is a technique for re-thatching an existing roof. The thatcher prepares a small handful of straw in the same way as a yealm. This is then fixed to the roof by lifting up a small section of the old thatch, hooking the new straw bundle over the end of a wooden swallow tail and tucking it under the old thatch leaving 6 or 8 inches showing. The thatcher works along the eaves as before and starts the next row 6 or 8 inches higher up. Stobbing is now no longer practised in this area. It relied on the original fixings of the old thatch to be in good repair. It was quicker than the other methods outlined above and may well have been popular for running repairs. It was certainly cheaper, the new layer of straw on a stobbed roof is only a few inches thick.

Chimneys and gutters.

One of the weakest points in a thatched roof is around the chimney. This is also one of the greatest fire hazards. Normally the thatch is butted up to the chimney stack and the join between stack and thatch is covered in a thick layer of mortar, lead is only occasionally used.

Most thatched roofs do not have gutters. The thatch projects beyond the house walls throwing the rain water well away from them. This creates a strip of bare ground all the way around the house because the constant dripping of water inhibits the growth of plants. This is most noticeable in flower beds.

An old complaint of thatched roofs was that they harbour unwanted livestock -mice,spiders,birds etc.A law passed in the reign of Elizabeth the first offered a bounty for every sparrow killed. This bounty came to be know as sparrow money. The law was passed in an effort to stop small birds eating the unthreshed corn in corn stacks and to stop them damaging thatched house roofs by nesting in them. In the past old fishing nets were sometimes used to prevent birds getting into the thatch. Over the last 100 years the problem has been largely overcome by a covering of fine mesh wire netting on the outside and various forms of cladding on the inside."we hear a bit of scratting

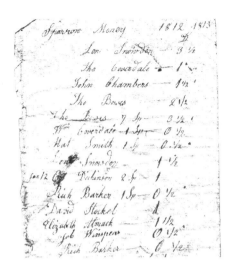

A list of payments of Sparrow money made to young children at Harome in 1812/3 discovered when moving Harome Manor House to the Ryedale Folk Museum. They were paid a halfpenny for every sparrow.

occasionally but it doesn't worry us" said one owner. Not that even one inch wire netting deters a determined wren. Mr Puffett of Pockley regularly has two pairs which find a way to enter and build a nest in his carefully netted roof and a young Tawny owl excavated a winter roost in the gable of the Manor House at the Ryedale Folk Museum. Most thatched roofs in Ryedale are now netted. The netting tends to trap small particles of debris and moisture and this in turn encourages mosses and lichens to establish themselves far more quickly. Thick accumulations of mosses and lichens will have a tendency to rot the straw. Reed thatch is normally dense and hard enough to deter bird damage and is not normally wired.

Wren.
Troglodgtes troglodgtes

GAZETTEER

Ainthorpe

Hajoles cottage in the centre of the Eskdale village of Ainthorpe is unique in having been totally remade. From humble beginnings as a pighouse attached to a barn on Beech Farm, it escaped modernisation until the late 1970's when its original floor to ceiling cruck and ancient thatched roof had acquired historical significance. The ruinous building-tin-roofed over decayed thatch - was completely dismantled and rebuilt with new foundations on the original site. This may well be the only moorland cruck thatched cottage standing damp-free on concrete footings. Its wheat straw thatch was replaced with Norfolk reed in 1990.

Beadlam

Rose Cottage has been home to the Bumby family for nigh on 100 years. Its multi-layered thatch provides exceptionally wide overhang to rear windows. In non-decorative style, the thatch seems to complement the charm of a surrounding traditional cottage garden.

White Cottage, only a stone's throw from Rose Cottage, shows a contrasting modern style with block cut ridge. Criss-cross arrangement of eave and ridge hazel spars is augmented by a part curved gable end and a pair of straw birds strutting along the ridge. An old custom of whitened walls- supposedly to deter insect and rodent pests - has been maintained at the front of this cottage.

Cliff Cottage is a traditional longhouse with through passage and attached cow byre, now incorporated into domestic use. The white wall custom is maintained here also. Thatched in the early 1970's with wheat straw, it has recently been re-thatched with rye and retains rare gable boards.

Bilsdale

Broadway Foot. When in 1987 this ancient farmhouse was totally stripped of successive thatch layers up to 6ft thick it was found that the chimney stack had been raised to accommodate the deeper thatch. It took seven months to thatch a new roof with reed. The straw ridge was netted as were the gable ends. Birds have dislodged bits of the supposedly impenetrable and unnetted reed. Originally a longhouse on the Duncome estate, this dwelling is one of the oldest in the dale and may be on the site of an early monastic building. It has undergone extensive renovation in recent decades and is one of two remaining thatched properties in Bilsdale.

Spout House, formerly the old Sun Inn, fell into disrepair when a new inn was built nearby in 1914. Much dilapidated but still more or less intact, the building was leased by the National Park in 1979 and, restored to its original state, it is now open to the public. Six tons of rye straw grown at Wilberfoss near York, were used to cover the old thatch. Original 'thackbands' of woven straw fastened to roofing spars are visible in the bedrooms. Spout House is thought to have been built in 1550 on the site of a previous cottage thus its stone walls may be replacements for earlier timber framing using crucks dating back to the 16th century or before.

Carlton Husthwaite

Thatched Cottage probably dating from Tudor times, is typical of early houses in the Vale of York more than Ryedale. A black and white timbered cruck house built single-storied open to the thatched roof, its upstairs rooms were inserted later. It was substantially restored in 1967 with a reed roof and wheat straw ridge. Its hipped roof has a scalloped pattern cut at the ridge and shaved into the roof above the eaves.

Egton

Crossview Cottage was being re-thatched in 1998 Before this work started, the ravages of time and weather showed in weeds and moss sprouting from the old roof with serious water penetration and bird damage. This single storey cottage adjoins a pantiled cottage and has the only remaining thatched roof in Egton. It was for many years clad with a corrugated iron roof.

Delves Cottage in a hamlet south of Egton, is a single-storey longhouse with cross passage, probably built in 1713, and has three full cruck trusses which are believed to be older than the walls. Two pairs of crucks reveal a single bay living area some 16ft x 12ft with former cattle housing incorporated to extend the cottage. Like many more, this cottage underwent a period with a corrugated iron roof before being re-thatched in 1976 and again in 1994.

Farndale

Oak House is a rare example of a two storey dwelling pleasingly supporting a traditional thatch. A straw owl perches neatly on a partly scalloped ridge and a sloping eaves line blends into adjacent pantile roofs.

Oak Crag, Farndale west, was one of the oldest cottages in the dale, with with ancient wood panelling, heck post and screen. Sadly it was destroyed by fire in the 1970's. A new house now stands on the site.

Hollins farm, Dale End - Part of this house now has a corrugated asbestos roof. Its steep pitch indicates previous thatch.

Harome

Star Inn - Thatched in the 1960's by two thatchers from Suffolk, this roof has lasted nearly 40 years and was being re-thatched with wheat straw in 1999. This building has a reputation of being the only remaining thatched inn in north east Yorkshire. Certainly it boasts the only thatched public toilet in the North York Moors.

Black Eagle - a derelict cottage at the east end of the village was formerly whitewashed and for many years roofed with corrugated iron over dilapidated wheat straw. Once two tiny cottages with rooms no more than 10ft square and earthern or stone flagged floors, the building has crucks and roof timbers with thatch exposed to the rooms below. Fire grates and a lean-to outhouse added a modicum of comfort to these humble homes which were occupied until only a decade or two ago. It has recently changed hands and is to be renovated and re-thatched in 1999.

Orchard House in Harome main street had a new covering of wheat straw thatch in 1998. Its decorative cut ridge shows a different more 'chocolate box' style used by a thatcher new to the district.

The Farm in the village street has had its straw roof patched and repaired more than once in the past 20 years; the initial cost of a thatched roof was in days gone by a good deal less than pantiles, but both this and the cost of maintaining thatch now far exceed that of tiles.

Holly Cottage, Mill Lane, has recently had a new thatch covering complete with straw owl and pheasant on a raised decorative ridge. Scottish water reed was capped with a ridge of wheat straw. Unusual for Ryedale a pink render covers the front wall although the rear retains traditional white.This part single and part double storied cottage has a 3ft overhang of thatch at the eaves indicating numerous layers of thatch.

Mill Cottage was given a new rye straw covering on its back roof and raised ridge a few years ago. Upstairs rooms have been created in the roof space with dormer windows placed back from the exterior wall and opening on to wide tiled cills.

Mill Cottage Harome. Thatch several feet thick has required the chimney to be extended.

Mill Green has retained an old thatched building alongside a modern two-storey house with thatched porch. A sequence of building styles is depicted by this small terrace with the original cottage nestling between its stone built extension on one side and a substantial brick house on the other. The old cottage has two of the smallest possible windows barely more than a foot square peeping through its thatch just above eaves height.

Hutton-le-Hole

The four reconstructed cottages at Ryedale Folk Museum show how thatching has changed through the ages.

Crofters cottage is the type of home of a medieval peasant scraping a meagre living from his small garth and farm labouring. He would have built and roofed the cottage himself using local materials - wood, clay and stones with turf, straw, heather and bracken for the roof.

1630 The Manor House was removed from Harome where it had been the Tudor home of a manorial lord. Sturdy timbers clad with superior rye straw were used for this prestigious building which would have served as home, courtroom and meeting hall.

1704 Stang End is a more humble dwelling. Removed from Danby in Eskdale, it is typical of small farmsteads scattered throughout the area. Generations of peasant families reared cattle, pigs, poultry etc, housed a workhorse or two, tilled a few nearby fields and wove bolts of wool or linen cloth in this dwelling and adjacent outbuildings.
Local materials were used for construction with easily renewable heather and turf for the roof covering.

1870 White Cottage, also removed from Harome, shows a more affluent home built more than two centuries later than the Manor house and situated in a thriving lowland village off the moors. Wheat straw was then available and a good appearance was required as well as a comfortable home.

Leavening

Middle Field Farm was for many years known as 'Tin Tops' on account of the corrugated iron which covered its decayed thatch. In the 1980's it acquired a new owner who had it re-thatched with rye straw and renovated the old farmhouse along with adjacent buildings to create a substantial holiday complex. In keeping with the ancient farmhouse, an old tree nearby has been given a new lease of life by a massive support to its leaning trunk.

The White Cottage from Harome reconstructed at the Ryedale Folk Museum.

Old Malton

Little Thatch, Westgate provides an intriguing example of changing living standards. An observer at the turn of the century described cottages in Old Malton as 'very old, roofed with thatch tiny, dark and damp' [Royal Commission - Houses of the North York Moors].

Today this cottage is a stylish comfortable home with decorative thatch superimposed on the old, new windows, a staircase and upstairs rooms creating a standard of living undreamt of a century ago.

Thatch Cottage also in Westgate is the only other remaining thatched property in Old Malton. It too has been modernised to meet todays standards with windows for upstairs rooms tucked in beneath overhanging thatch. The reed roof has a wheat straw ridge.

Pockley

White Cottage is an ancient longhouse with an unusual hipped and upturned gable end. Centuries ago it would have provided shelter for a farming family and their livestock. Recent patching on the roof is a reminder that upkeep of a watertight roof is an ongoing problem for thatch owners. Triticale, a hybrid which combines the length of rye with the durability of wheat has been used on this roof.

The Old Forge has a steep thatch, modestly trimmed with hazel spars, which blends well with tiled extensions. Gable ends reveal successive thatch layers.

The Old Forge Pockley with a traditional long straw roof.

Low Farm has lead flashing round its chimney stacks - presumably to avoid a recurrence of the fire which ravaged this roof some 20 years ago. Here the problem of light to upstairs rooms has been met by modern flat roofed dormers, but thatch has been retained on the 'catslide' roof of a lean-to extension.

The Moorings housed the village post office in the 1980's. A sturdy batten near the gable end suggests a strategy to prevent wind raising the thatch in this exposed location.

The Moorings Pockley. A new block cut ridge has been added. Note the sturdy batten down the gable.

Daleside is another traditional longhouse with wooden battens giving added protection to the wheat straw roof. Protection of a different sort was sought by a fox once seen by the cottage owner. In a desperate attempt to escape from the hounds, the fox climbed up the thatched roof, ran smartly along the ridge and disappeared down the chimney!

West View is a cottage where stout straps have been used to secure the thatch at a windy gable end. In common with several other properties, the roof above the kitchen has been tiled, presumably to minimise fire risk. Tiles also enable insertion of a roof light to augment a small upper gable end window.

Brecks Cottage is a new house built in Pockley in 1998. It was thatched with water reed from Turkey and ridged with Yorkshire grown rye straw. A modern innovation in this building is the insertion of a fire retardant membrane between the roof timbers and the thatch.

Rievaulx

Rose Cottage has a gable end of thatch cut off in line with the wall beneath. This exposes a clear profile of at least four layers of thatch - now so thick that the roof looks almost too heavy for the cottage to carry. The scallop cut ridge tapers to a pinnacle above the gable. The older and thatched part of Rose cottage is single storied in contrast to a later two- storey extension with tiled roof.

43

Swiss Cottage Rievaulx with a rolled gable, that gives added security to the thatch.
There is such a great thickness of thatch that the chimney has had to be extended.

Swiss Cottage acquired a new thatch covering in 1994 at a cost of £8000. Rye straw was bought from farms at Holme-on-Spalding Moor and Staintondale. In contrast to a thatched cottage across the road, the gable end of the thatch has been rolled over to conceal previous layers - a style more familiar in East Anglia than Ryedale.

Runswick Bay -

this cottage by the sea was formerly an estate office and is now a holiday cottage only a stone's throw from the sea - . so close that all thatching material had to be wheelbarrowed in from the nearest track! Its recently renewed roof is made from Scottish water reed topped with sedge (*Cladium mariscus*) brought from Wicken Fen, a nature reserve in Cambridgeshire. This material was used to provide longer protection against the salt air than straw would have done. To minimise damage from wind and birds, the roof is covered with wire netting. A further protective device is the erection of three upstanding strands of wire above the ridge to prevent seagulls from perching.

A Cottage right on the edge of the sea at Runswick Bay thatched by William Tegetmeir in Scottish water Reed.

Scackleton

at Roundhill Court in this small hamlet on the Howardian Hills a builder in 1994 erected two 'executive style' houses with intricate thatched roofs - a far cry from the small scale cottage normally associated with thatch. Thatchers from Manchester used Scottish reed for the roofs with wheat straw on decorative ridges, lead flashings round windows and chimneys but no spars visible along the eaves.

Scarborough

in Stepney Drive stands a unique property which featured as House of the Year at the Ideal Homes exhibition in 1938. It was built on site in London then dismantled and re-built in Scarborough. Its art-deco design incorporates a leaded flat roof as well as ridged and part circular roofs thatched with Norfolk reed. Wheat straw ridges have been renewed but the original reed thatch has lasted 60 years.

Snainton

The only remaining thatched property between Thornton le Dale and the coast, this two-storied house in the main street at Snainton was for many years covered with sheets of corrugated iron. It was rethatched with reed and a wheat straw ridge by a thatcher from Manchester.

Sproxton

Forge Cottage - dormer windows on an upper floor create an interesting eaves line for the thatch on this restored old cottage. At the pinnacled gable end can be seen a succession of thatch layers showing a mixture of rye and wheat straw.

Thornton-le-Dale

Beck Isle Cottage with its stream-side setting and backdrop of trees presents a truly romantic picture of a thatched cottage. It was formerly the Hill estate office when like many others its walls were whitewashed. It fell into dereliction and was rescued and restored by a local doctor. Now a private house, it is much visited and photographed. When last re-thatched Hungarian water reed was used. A lorry load was driven direct from Hungary by a Hungarian long-distance driver who spoke no English but eventually found his way to Thornton-le-Dale! Because the cottage stands near the edge of Thornton Beck, the thatcher spent a good deal of time wading to move his ladder along the stream bed.

Perhaps the most photographed thatched building in the area Beck Isle Cottage Thornton -le - Dale c 1930. It is being thatched in the local long straw tradition. Photo Hayes RFM1629. Compare this with photo on page 47.

Beck Isle cottage in 1998. The white wash has all gone and note the scalloped ridge and new dormer windows.

Warter

This 19th century terrace of estate workers' cottages were part re-thatched in 1998 by thatchers from Manchester. New cut ridges with pinnacles were constructed over porches, gabled dormers and the main roof.

BIBLIOGRAPHY

Life in the Moorlands of North-East Yorkshire by Marie Hartley and Joan
    Ingilby published by J M Dent & Sons Ltd 1972
The Pattern of English Building by Alec Clifton-Taylor published Faber &
    Faber 1972
English Building Construction by C F Innocent published by David and
    Charles 1971
Vernacular Houses iin North Yorkshire and Cleveland by Barry Harrison and
    Barbara Hutton published by John Donald Publishers Ltd 1984
A History of Goathland by Alice Hollings published by North York Moors
    National Park
Houses of the North York Moors by Royal Commission on the Historical
    Monuments (England) 1987
Dalesman September 1983, February 1961
Thatch and Thatching by Jacqueline Fearn published by Shire Publications
Ryedale Recipes by Peter Brears 1998
North Yorkshire County Record Office - Feversham Estate papers
                                       Levisham parish records
                                       Middleton churchwardens' accounts
Minute book of Kirkbymoorside Preparative Quaker Meeting